My Emotions
Emosyon Mwen Yo

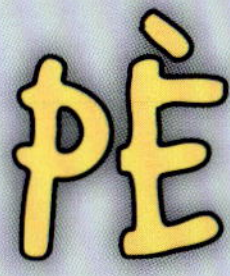

A Crabtree Roots Book
Yon Liv Crabtree Rasin

AMY CULLIFORD
JEAN-PIERRE GASTON

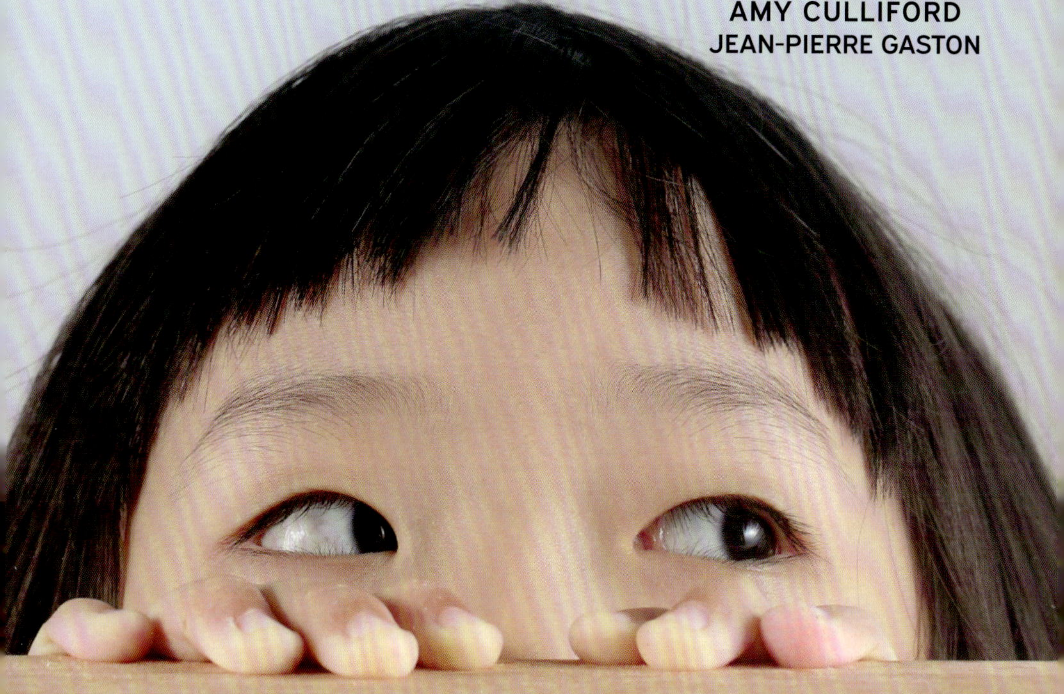

Crabtree Publishing
crabtreebooks.com

School-to-Home Support for Caregivers and Teachers

This book helps children grow by letting them practice reading. Here are a few guiding questions to help the reader with building his or her comprehension skills. Possible answers appear here in red.

Before Reading:

- What do I think this book is about?
    - *This book is about feeling scared.*
    - *This book is about what feeling scared looks or feels like.*

- What do I want to learn about this topic?
    - *I want to learn what to do if I feel scared.*
    - *I want to learn what feeling scared looks like.*

During Reading:

- I wonder why...
    - *I wonder why we cry when we are scared.*
    - *I wonder why trying new things is scary.*

- What have I learned so far?
    - *I have learned that scared is an emotion.*
    - *I have learned that some people yell when they are scared.*

After Reading:

- What details did I learn about this topic?
    - *I have learned that it is good to tell someone you are scared.*
    - *I have learned that everyone can feel scared about something.*

- Read the book again and look for the vocabulary words.
    - *I see the word **hide** on page 6 and the word **storms** on page 8. The other vocabulary words are found on page 14.*

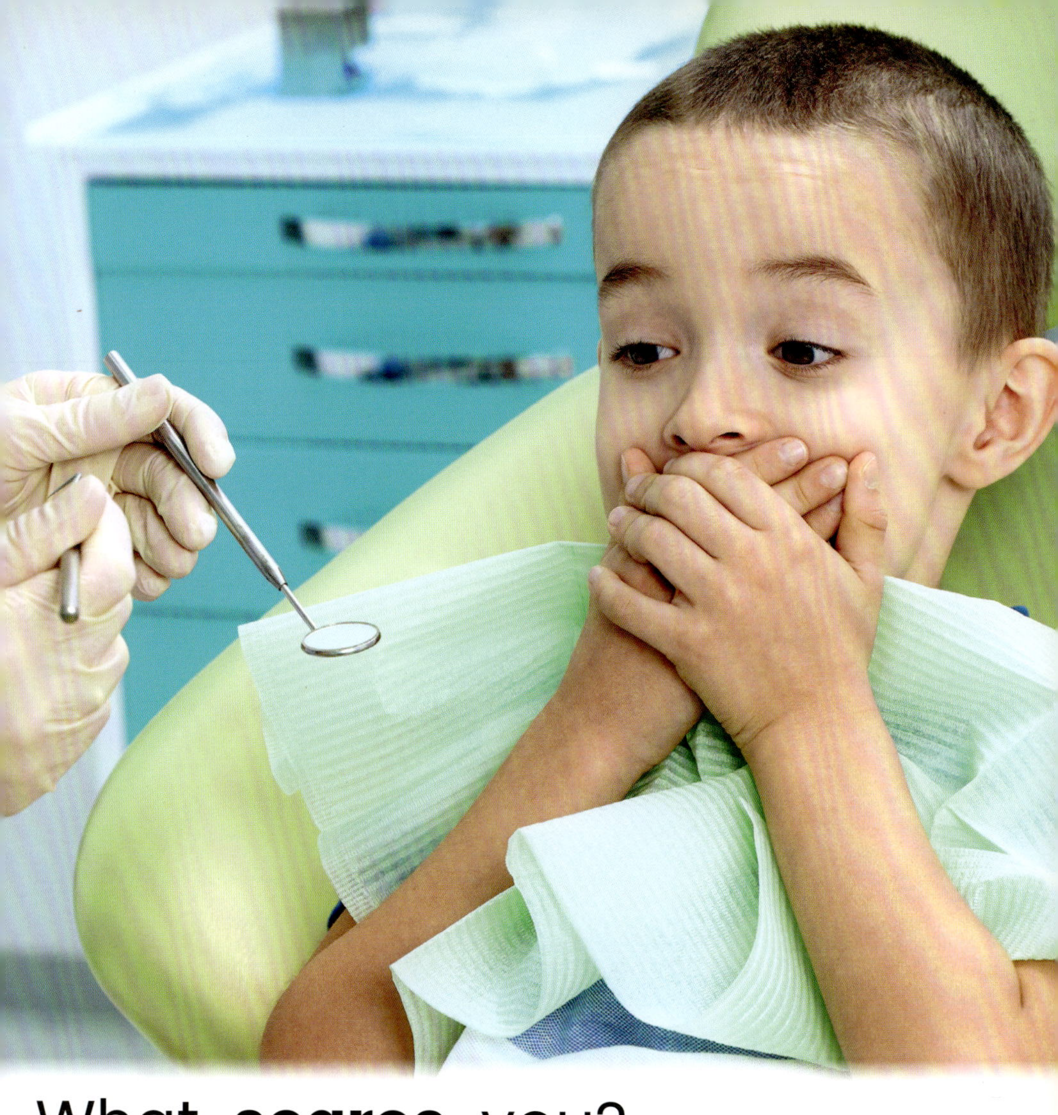

What **scares** you?

Ki sa ki fè ou **pè**?

I am scared of the **dark**.

Mwen pè nan fè **nwa**.

I **hide** when I am scared.

Mwen ale **kache** lè mwen pè.

I am scared of **storms**.

Mwen pè **tanpèt**.

I **cry** when am I am scared.

Mwen **kriye** lè mwen pè.

I go find my **mom** when I am scared.

Mwen ale jwenn **manman** mwen lè mwen pè.

What scares you?

Ki sa ki fè ou pè?

Words to Know
Mo pouw Konnen

cry
kriye

dark
nwa

hide
kache

mom
manman

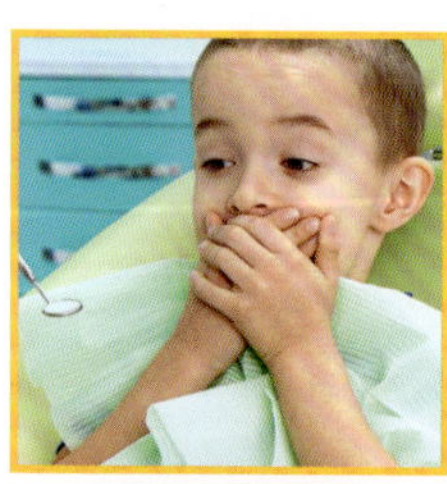

scares
pè

storms
tonpèt

38 Words

What **scares** you?

I am scared of the **dark**.

I **hide** when I am scared.

I am scared of **storms**.

I **cry** when I am scared.

I go find my **mom** when I am scared.

What scares you?

38 mo

Kisa ki fè ou **pè**?

Mwen pè nan fè **nwa**.

Mwen ale **kache** lè mwen pè.

Mwen pè **tanpèt**.

Mwen **kriye** lè mwen pè.

Mwen ale jwenn **manman** mwen lè mwen pè.

Ki sa ki fè ou pè?

My Emotions

Emosyon Mwen Yo

Written by: Amy Culliford

Designed by: Rhea Wallace

Series Development: James Earley

Proofreader: Ellen Rodger

Educational Consultant: Marie Lemke M.Ed.

Photographs:
Shutterstock: Juan Pablo Gonzaález: cover; TY Ilm: p. 1; Aleksandr Rybalko: p. 3, 14; Kryzhov: p. 5, 14; justoomm: p. 7, 14; HelloRF Zcool: p. 8, 14; fizkes: p. 9, 14; Inna Ska: p. 13

Crabtree Publishing

crabtreebooks.com 800-387-7650

Copyright © 2023 Crabtree Publishing
All rights reserved. No part of this publication may be reproduced, stored in a retrieval system or be transmitted in any form or by any means, electronic, mechanical, photocopying, recording, or otherwise, without the prior written permission of Crabtree Publishing Company.

Printed in Printed in China/082022/FE052422CT

Published in Canada
Crabtree Publishing
616 Welland Ave.
St. Catharines, Ontario
L2M 5V6

Published in the United States
Crabtree Publishing
347 Fifth Avenue,
Suite 1402-145
New York, NY, 10016

Library and Archives Canada Cataloguing in Publication
Available at the Library and Archives Canada

Library of Congress Cataloging-in-Publication Data
Available at the Library of Congress

Paperback: 9781039624603
Ebook: 9781039625440
Epub: 9781039625020